You Can Do All Things

Workbook

Dr. Jake Schmitz

INSTRUCTIONS

This book is a workbook and a companion to the main book "You Can Do All Things." What I recommend is you read the main book first, and then re-read it and do the accompanying exercises in this workbook. You now have a roadmap and a system to make your life better than you ever imagined!

You CAN Do All Things.

CONTENTS

CHAPTER 1 EXERCISES

1.   Do you have any fear of failure that plagues your mind? What are they? In order to overcome, you need to be clear what the problem is, so write it down.

_____

_____

_____

_____

_____

_____

_____

_____

_____

2.   What are you past failures trying to teach you? What lesson is there, waiting for you to decipher?

Spend focused time on unlocking the lesson your subconscious is trying to teach you! This will give you the power to move on, leaving this fear behind you.

3. Are you, like I was, afraid of success, and how it will change who you are currently?

    One simple exercise that will help with this fear is to spend time on all the things you will gain by achieving your goals. Write out how your life will get better, not worse, by dominating your fear. Maybe it is more time, success, money, relationships, etc.

    Write out your list and put focused energy into all the positives! This will overrule all the negative that creeps into your mind.

_____

_____

_____

_____

_____

_____

4. What are your "time vampires"? What thing, or things, are currently stealing your time? Write down those activities (and be honest) that you spend your time doing each day that, if reallocated, would be better invested in moving you towards your goal or aspirations? How much time are you wasting each day?

_____

_____

_____

_____

_____

5. Having a fear of time can only work against you when you haven't taken the first step to write out a projected timeline of how long your goal should take to complete!

Write out both a long term projection and a short term projection with a completion date. This will give you a range to better appreciate how long it should take.

_____

_____

_____

_____

_____

_____

_____

_____

6.   Now, take that goal, and chunk it down to bite size pieces you can accomplish with time lines. This will keep you motivated along the path to ultimate success!

_____

_____

_____

_____

_____

_____

_____

_____

_____

7.   The fear of rejection is one of the, if not the, hardest fears to overcome! This fear can manifest itself as any of the other fears, as well. That being said, the easiest and most effective way to change from fear to power is to apply this saying, "What is the worst thing that could happen?" This puts perspective on your situation, and brings a sense of reality that is usually lacking with this fear. Write out the "worst case".

_____

_____

_____

_____

_____

_____

8.   that you have the "worst case", write out the "best case", or best possible outcome to this situation. This will give you the incentive to try, even though the fear is still present!

_____

_____

_____

_____

_____

_____

9.   What is your rejection number? How many "no's" do you have to hear to get your first "yes"?

_____

_____

_____

_____

_____

CHAPTER 2 EXERCISES

1.   Self-esteem is the value or worth you place on yourself. In what way(s) have you let others decrease or question your self-worth? Write out all the things that cause you to question your self-worth.

_____

_____

_____

_____

_____

2.   When you look at this list of things that causes you to question your self-worth, are there commonalities between them? Is there a consistent message that keeps surfacing, your limiting belief; i.e. too old, too young, too fat, too poor, etc.? When you see the message the next step is to write its opposite, positive statement. "I'm too old" becomes "I am the perfect age, with wisdom and experience a plenty, to achieve success in all I do!" Write out your new empowering belief statement!

_____

_____

_____

_____

3.   Meditate on this every day. Repeat your empowering belief statement out loud, with conviction, (as if you were trying to convince your neighbor) every day, 3-5 times per day. It is also good to say this anytime you feel your self-esteem wavering! This will give you the spiritual power to overcome any doubt that tries to creep over you!

CHAPTER 3 EXERCISES

1. Ego can be one of the hardest self-defeating traits a person needs to eliminate! In what ways does your ego rear its ugly head? Are you compensating for your lack of self-confidence? Write down all the areas in your life (work, home, church, etc.) where your ego shows up.

_____

_____

_____

_____

_____

_____

2. Choose your 3-5 closest advisors to help you with the next part. Have them rate you on a scale of 0-10. 0 is having no ego (Mother Teresa), and 10 being the most egotistical, obnoxious person on the planet. How do you rate in other people's eyes? What emotions are present when you look at your results? Write out 3 ways you could change from ego to self-confidence.

_____

_____

_____

_____

3.   Create a victory wall. Put up pictures, words, anything that gives you an association to positive emotions of confidence. It can be anything in which you felt successful. Look at your victory wall every day!

4.   What negative emotions have you been accepting as truth(s)? How do you feel when you think of these emotions? Write out those negative emotions and their associated feelings.

_____

_____

_____

_____

_____

_____

5.   What are the opposite positive emotions? Write about an experience you have had in your life that made you feel the opposite of your negative emotion; i.e. you feel sad, think of an experience that gave you the most joy. You feel scared, what event made you feel powerful?

_____

_____

_____

_____

_____

_____

6.   Compliment yourself! To start your day off in the right direction, say five compliments about yourself before you even get out of bed!

CHAPTER 4 EXERCISES

1.   What event(s) in your life have caused regret? What happened to cause this feeling? How did you respond or react to the situation? What has transpired in the wake of this event? How has this event shaped your expectations of the future? Write it out, preferably in story format. Paint the picture so that if someone reads it, they would feel as if they were there!

_____

_____

_____

_____

_____

_____

_____

_____

_____

2. Now that it is out on paper, you need to analyze the situation. Was there something you could have done differently to avoid what happened?

Were your actions the cause of the situation? What role did you play in the situation? How could you have stopped it from happening? Write your answers using story format again. However, this time do it from an unbiased, third-party perspective, as if you were reading this story, and needed to give solutions to what happened.

This will give insight on how you could have handled it differently (if, in fact, you could have done it differently!)

_____

_____

_____

_____

3. What is the truth in this situation? I love this question, because it cuts right to the heart of the problem! Are there areas in your life (work, family, etc.) that seem to consistently go wrong (or at least not the way you wanted or planned)? Why is that? Again, what is the truth in this situation? Is it something you keep messing up? Is your boss, co-worker, spouse, child, etc. just not understanding you? Do you need more clarity? How can you change your response to this issue?

You cannot change someone else! You can only change yourself, which will have an impact on the other person. In what ways can you change?

_____

_____

_____

4. Now actually change! You see the problem, and you know the truth, so just change! When you change yourself (or those areas in your life where deficiencies remain/occur), you can change the world!

CHAPTER 5 EXERCISES

1. Are you the absolute best at what you do in your organization? Is there someone better? If there is someone better, what did he/she do to become the best? Ask them to help you! If they can do it, so can you.

2. Do you have a coach? All the best people in any area (sports, work, church, etc.) have coaches or mentors to help along the path to success. Who would be a good coach/mentor for you? How much improvement is possible for you with a little tweaking? How much farther could your grow with the right advice? Find a coach/mentor to help you on your journey!

3. Self-training is one of the most important factors in any industry. Your personal growth is predicated by the amount of training you are willing to do! There is a seemingly limitless growth potential in life, but people often get stagnant. Growth is stunted by an attitude of "Its good enough." We stop training, stop growing, and stop learning because we fall back on routine. In what ways can you start training yourself again? Write those ways down, and commit yourself to apply them!

_____

_____

_____

_____

_____

CHAPTER 6 EXERCISES

1. Plot out your "time map". Once written on paper, evaluate how much extra time you think you would now have? For the first couple of weeks, this will change frequently, but once you get a handle on your time, you can be quite accurate. This will be sobering reminder of how much time you truly do have in a day!

2. Each day write out your note card! What three to five things must get done today? How will that (getting your top priorities accomplished) affect your current stress levels? When you consistently get things done, your stress levels naturally go down! Write your note card!

3. I remember as a child the worst words my parents said to me was "bedtime." I hated being forced to go to sleep at a set time! My parents always told me I would feel better if I went to sleep early. I did not believe them. Now, as an adult, I fully appreciate "bedtime". Do you have a "bedtime"? Are you getting enough sleep? You cannot be your best self when you are always tired! Set a good "bedtime" so you are well rested!

CHAPTER 7 EXERCISES

1.   Do you have a goal or goals you are trying to achieve? Have you written it on paper? This is where you do that! In my book you read that goals have to be specific, measurable, achievable, relevant, and time-bound. Go ahead and write out your goal(s), in the space provided. Make sure your goals have these five criteria!

_____

_____

_____

_____

_____

_____

_____

2.   Now that your goals are on paper, put it someplace you will review it EVERY DAY! This reviewing process solidifies your goal in your mind, and sets you creative juices flowing towards their achievement! Have fun with this. By reviewing your goals every day, it becomes easy to see which activities you do each day that push you toward your goal, and which ones pull you off track! Your job is to then maximize the good ones and minimize or eliminate the negative ones. This will shoot you like a rocket towards the completion of your goals!

CHAPTER 8 EXERCISES

1.   Affirmations are great way to improve mood, increase confidence and manufacture successful interactions at work/home/life due to a better mental state!

Do you practice affirmations? If not, why not? When is the best time to plant a tree? 20 years ago. When is the second best time? Right now! Start speaking words of power and encouragement to yourself! Choose the area(s) in your life where you need a confidence boost.

Write out three to five positive statements, which start with "I am ......", "I will.....", "I have...." etc. Always frame it in the positive, as if you have already achieved your statement!

2.   Going hand-in-hand with positive affirmations are positive visualizations! Visualization is an exercise that entails viewing your event (or day) in its "best possible outcome". When viewing it this way, you need to believe in your spirit that it will actually happen the way you want it to.

This goes a long way to ensuring you will have the best outcomes everyday to come. At first it is hard to do but with practice, it becomes easier to do. Make it fun, because it should be fun visualizing the best day of your life!

CHAPTER 9 EXERCISES

1.   What are you passionate about? What one thing would you do, no matter what anyone thinks? If you got paid to do it, would you quit your job to follow? Spend some quality alone time, meditating on what that thing is, and how you could do that as a means of income! Keep in mind, people will think you are crazy, but who really cares? You are following YOUR PASSION!

2.   What skills do you have that come naturally to you? These are specifically gifted to you in order to achieve your God-ordained mission! Are you using your gifts? Or are you like many people who go to a dead-end job every day, where you are not utilizing your gifting? How can you start utilizing your gifts today in a productive way?

3.   Have you ever taken a personality test to determine where your best fit would be? There are dozens of websites that allow free tests, and even interpret them for you! Take a test, and find out how to use your personality to its fullest potential!

4.   What fires you up? In what area or situation do you have a "holy discontent"? How could your natural talents or gifts affect this situation for the betterment of others? Write out how you could be the solution to this situation, which will point you in the direction of your passionate calling!

_____

_____

_____

_____

_____

_____

CHAPTER 10 EXERCISES

1.   Do you have a mission or cause you are passionately fighting for? Are you "all-in" to the fulfillment of that cause? If not, why not? Write down 2-3 ways you could put yourself more on the front lines to have a greater impact!

_____

_____

_____

_____

_____

_____

2.   Evaluate the time allocation choices you make every day. How could you change some of your everyday choices to improve or increase with your mission?

_____

_____

_____

_____

_____

3.   What are your distractions? Where are you losing time? How could you, by eliminating some bad choices, free up hours a day to be used more effectively?

_____

_____

_____

_____

_____

_____

_____

CHAPTER 11 EXERCISES

1. It takes 10,000 hours to develop to the level of master in any field or industry. How close or far are you from achieving your 10,000 hours? How can you increase your time investment right now to hit your 10,000 hours? How can you increase your time investment right now to hit your 10,000 hours sooner? Write out your plan as to how you will achieve your 10,000 hours

_____

_____

_____

_____

_____

_____

_____

_____

2.   Training is the best way to get ahead in any area in life, whether it is in athletics, health, fitness, work, etc. training can get you to mastery faster, and keep you on top longer! Larry Bird trained extra hours a day to get and stay on top.

How are you going to do extra training to get ahead of your competition?

_____

_____

_____

_____

_____

_____

3.   Masters are masters because they have higher standards for quality than anyone else. How can you increase your current quality of work to another level?

_____

_____

_____

_____

4.   Where are your blind spots? Everyone has them. Some are worse (or bigger) than others. Who in your life is pointing out your blind spots? Unless you are paying them to do so, your friends or family are not the ones to point out blind spots for you! You need an unbiased, third party to point them out. That is what a coach will do for you! You pay them to point out your bad B.S. (belief systems)! If you do not currently have a coach, find one! It will be the best investment you could ever make!

CHAPTER 12 EXERCISES

1.   Are you the voice of your mission? If you were the last one left (with this mission) would your mission survive? In what ways could you increase your voice, so as to be heard by more people? Write your thought down.

_____

_____

_____

_____

_____

2.   Martin Luther King, Jr. lived according to a set of core principles. What are you core values or principles? What code do you live by? If you have never thought about it until now, that is okay. Take some time to figure out your core principles. Once you have them, write them out!

_____

_____

_____

_____

_____

3. Your core principles are what people will remember most about you after you are gone! That will be your legacy! Reflect on your life. What would people remember about you, as you live now? How long, after you are gone, would you be remembered? How can you start, right now, living your core values so people remember you for who you want to be remembered?

_____

_____

_____

_____

4. Do you make room for others to join your cause, or are you a one man/woman show? Where would your mission be if you allowed others to come on board? Martin Luther King, Jr. had a mission, but he could not do it alone! He mobilized others to help spread his mission farther. In what ways could you let others join you?

_____

_____

_____

_____

5. "Who you are speaks so loudly that I can't hear what you are saying." How are you representing your mission? You are a walking, talking billboard for your mission. Are people noticing your amazing mission? Or are they laughing at your incongruence? Martin Luther King, Jr. lived his passion all day, every day! Are you? If not, how could you start living it out in your life every day?

_____

_____

_____

_____

_____

_____